SHARKS!

PHONICS

Great Whites

Book 6: wh (Beginning blend)

Quinlan B. Lee

Photo Credits: cov... ...Alamy; title page: Keren Su/Corbis; page 2: BartCo/iStockphoto; pages 4-5: David Jenkins/Getty Images; pages 6... ...olle/Shutterstock; pages 8-9: Michael Patrick O'Neill/Alamy; pages 10-11: Mauricio Handler/National Geographic; pages 12-13: Keren Su/Corbis; pages 14-15: Brandon Cole Marine Photography/Alamy; page 16: Mike Parry/Minden Pictures.

ISBN 978-0-545-74704-2

12 11 10 9 8 7 6 5 4 3 2 1   14 15 16 17 18/0

Printed in China   145

First Printing, September 2014

SCHOLASTIC INC.

What is that in the water?

Some seals see it **whisk** by.

Whatever it is, the seals

keep swimming.

Wham!

A great **white** shark **whips** out of the water.

It grabs a seal!

Then it **whacks** back down with a splash.

Great **white** sharks are the biggest predators in the world. They can be as big as 20 feet long and 5,000 pounds!

They eat seals, sea lions, and fish.

They even eat dead **whales** they find in the water.

A great **white** shark is sneaky.

Its back is blue and gray.

When seals look down on it,

they think it is just water.

The belly of the shark is **white**. **When** fish look up at it, they think it is just light.

Great **whites** have a great sense of smell.
They can smell a **whiff** of blood from three miles away.

If they smell blood **while** they are swimming one way, they **whirl** around.
Watch out, fish!

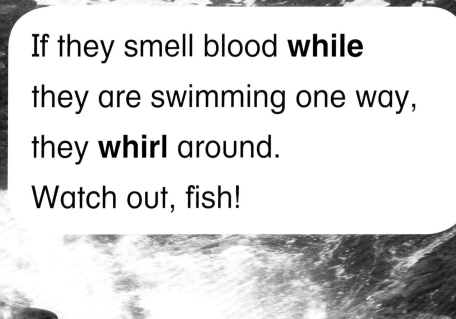

Great **whites** have a great sense of hearing.

They can hear a hurt seal's little **whimper**.

They will **whirl** around.
Then they will **whip** out of the
water to get it.
Watch out, seal!

Great **whites** do not eat people. But **when** people are near seals, great **whites** get confused.

Then they attack!
When a great **white**
realizes **what** it has bitten,
it swims away.

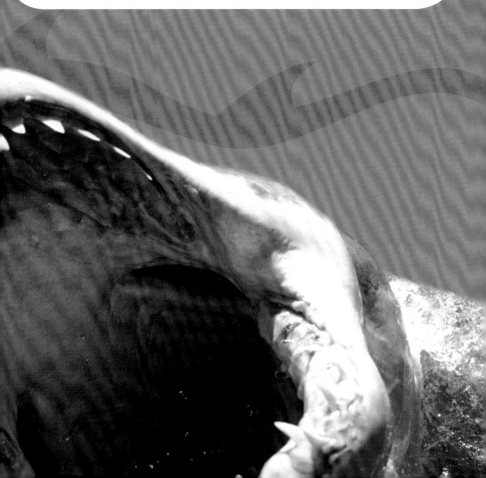

If you see a great **white**,
you should swim away, too!